CITY OF CULTURE

Montreal

JILL FORAN

Published by Weigl Educational Publishers Limited
6325 – 10 Street SE
Calgary, Alberta, Canada
T2H 2Z9
Web site: http://www.weigl.com

National Library of Canada Cataloguing in Publication Data
Foran, Jill.
Montreal

(Canadian Cities)
Includes Index
ISBN 1-894705-70-X

1. Montreal (Quebec)--Juvenile literature. I. Title. II. Series:
Canadian Cities (Calgary, Alta)
FC2947.33.F648 2001 j971.4'28 C2001-911387-0
F1054.5.M84F67 2001

Printed and bound in the United States of America
1 2 3 4 5 6 7 8 9 0 05 04 03 02 01

Senior Editor
Jared Keen
Copy Editor
Heather Kissock
Design
Warren Clark
Cover Design
Terry Paulhus
Layout
Bryan Pezzi
Photo Researcher
Tina Schwartzenberger

We acknowledge the financial support of the Government of Canada through the Book Publishing Industry Development Program (BPIDP) for our publishing activities.

Photograph Credits
Every reasonable effort has been made to trace ownership and to obtain permission to reprint copyright material. The publishers would be pleased to have any errors or omissions brought to their attention so that they may be corrected in subsequent printings.

Cover: Jean F. Leblanc/Agence Stock Photo; Inside Cover: Jean F. Leblanc/Agence Stock Photo; Normand Blouin/Agence Stock Photo: pages 3ML, 3TR, 5ML, 13T, 22, 27; Caroline Hayeur/Agence Stock Photo: pages 4, 5BR, 17B, 19, 24T, 26; Jean F. Leblanc/Agence Stock Photo: pages 11T, 14, 18T, 20T, 20B, 23BL, 29R, 30; Archives Nationales du Quebec, Centre de Montreal: pages 6T, 6B, 7M, 7B; A. Pichette/Bruce Bennett Studios: page 21T; Corel: pages 12B, 21B, 23T, 25; Geovisuals: pages 16, 24B; Jyde Heaven Photography: pages 3B, 12T, 13B, 15T, 15B, 29L; Courtesy of the Montreal Police Service: page 8T; National Archives of Canada: pages 8B (C-10721), 9M (PA-136711), 9B (C-18536), 10L (C-46600), 10T (C-47648), 18B (PA-166485), 28 (C-20126); PhotoDisc: page 17T; Photofest: page 11B.

Contents

Introduction

Montreal is the largest city in Quebec and also one of the oldest cities in Canada. It is located on Montreal Island, which lies in southern Quebec, near the **confluence** of the Saint Lawrence and Ottawa rivers. Montreal is a dynamic city and is known for its rich heritage, its beautiful architecture, and its friendly people.

Getting There

There are a number of ways to get to Montreal. Flights from all over the world arrive at Dorval International Airport every day. For those who prefer to drive or ride a bus, a network of highways connect to the city. You can also come by train or by boat.

At a Glanc

Climate

Montreal's climate varies a great deal throughout the year. The city's winters are usually quite snowy and cold, while its summers are often hot and humid. The average January temperatures in Montreal range from –5° Celsius to –15°C, and the average temperatures in July range from 15°C to 26°C. During autumn, the leaves on Montreal's many trees turn a fiery red, gold, and orange. During spring, beautiful flowers bloom throughout the city.

Area & Population

The city of Montreal covers an area of 177 square kilometres. About 1 million people live in the city, while about 3 million more live in its surrounding areas. In total, metropolitan Montreal consists of 102 municipalities, which encompass all of Montreal Island, as well as nearby islands and areas along the southern and northern shores of the Saint Lawrence River.

A Cosmopolitan City

Montreal has a strong French heritage. Settlers from France founded the city in 1642, and since then, it has become one of the country's main centres of French culture and language. As in most other areas of Quebec, the majority of Montreal's population is of French descent, and most residents speak French as their first language. French culture is a source of great pride and unity among the city's French Canadians. However, while French culture thrives in Montreal, the city is also home to many different ethnic groups that contribute to the rich **diversity** of the area. A significant number of Montrealers have English as their first language, which has created a distinctly bilingual atmosphere.

Interesting Statistics

1. Montreal is the largest French-speaking city in the world after Paris, France.

2. About 50 percent of the entire Quebec population lives in the Montreal Metropolitan Region.

3. Montreal's name is derived from Mount Royal, a mountain that sits in the middle of the city. At 230 m, Mount Royal is the city's highest point.

4. Montreal and its many surrounding communities are linked by more than twenty roads and railway bridges.

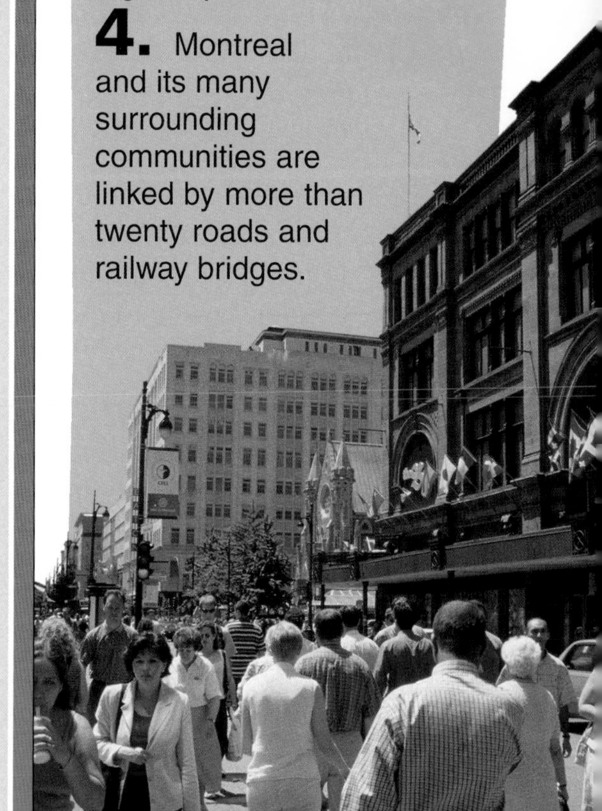

The Past

Early Settlement

A French explorer named Jacques Cartier was the first European known to visit what is now Montreal Island. He arrived in the area in 1535 and reportedly came across a **palisaded** village consisting of more than 1,000 Iroquois. This village was named Hochelaga, and it was located at the base of a mountain that Cartier named Mount Royal.

Montreal Island's first European settlement was also located at the base of Mount Royal. Called Ville Marie, this settlement was established in 1642 as a missionary colony. The settlement's founder was a Frenchman named Paul de Chomedey, Sieur de Maisonneuve. He brought with him about forty French settlers, and together they built homes, schools, a chapel, and a hospital. By the early 1700s, the mission of Ville Marie, which soon became known as Montreal, had developed into a prosperous French fur-trading centre.

In the early nineteenth century, Montreal was the political and commercial hub of Upper and Lower Canada.

Britain and France had been battling for control of the North American colonies for many years, and in 1760, Montreal surrendered to British forces. Britain now controlled Montreal, but it allowed the French settlers to keep their systems of law and government.

Key Events

1535 Jacques Cartier arrives in the Montreal area, where he encounters the Iroquois of Hochelaga and names Mount Royal.

Paul de Chomedey

1642 Paul de Chomedey, Sieur de Maisonneuve arrives on Montreal Island with forty French settlers, and Ville Marie is founded.

1760 Montreal surrenders to British Forces.

Government

Montreal became an official city in 1832. One year later, the first meeting of the new city council was held, and a man named Jacques Viger became the city's first mayor. When Montreal's **charter** expired in 1836, it was not renewed right away due to the political unrest that was developing throughout Lower Canada. Much of this unrest was due to tensions between French and British citizens. In 1837, Montreal became the scene of a rebellion against British subjects by a group of young **Francophones**. The rebellion settled down by the next year, and in 1840, Montreal was granted a new city charter. Four years later, the city became the capital of the United Province of Canada. It lost this position in 1849 after more riots led to a fire that destroyed the Parliament Building.

Although Montreal no longer served as the capital of Canada, it continued to grow at an incredible pace, and the municipal government grew with it. In 1851, a law was passed stating that the city's mayor was to be elected by the people. However, only those who owned property had the right to vote. It was not until more than a century later that the city's mayor and councillors were elected by all citizens, regardless of wealth. Under the guidance of early twentieth-century mayors such as Médéric Martin, Camillien Houde, and Jean Drapeau, Montreal continued to grow and prosper. Today, Montreal's city government consists of a mayor and fifty-one councillors.

Troops were called in from Upper Canada to end the Montreal Rebellion of 1837–1838.

1775 Montreal is occupied by American Revolutionary forces, who withdraw within months when an attempted siege on Quebec City fails.

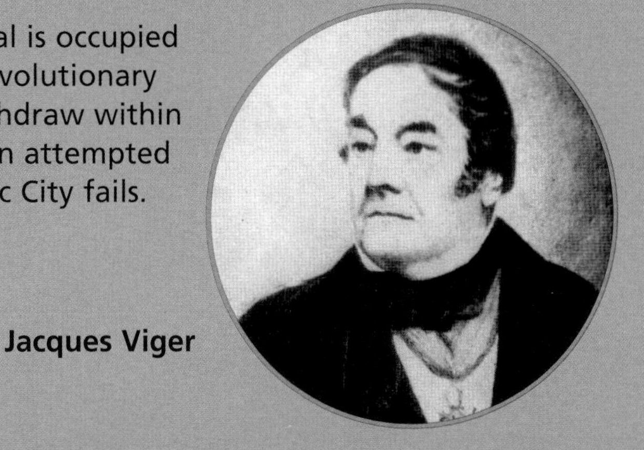

Jacques Viger

1820s Construction of the Lachine Canal is completed, and the city soon becomes a leading port.

1832 Montreal is incorporated as a city, and Jacques Viger becomes its first mayor.

Law and Order

Montreal's policing system dates back to the 1660s, when a militia of 100 volunteers was established to protect the inhabitants of Ville Marie. This militia was responsible for defending Ville Marie against invaders, but it had no power to enforce laws.

In 1730, Montreal formed a civil police force. Its volunteer members were responsible for protecting the townspeople as well as for bringing accused offenders to court. For the rest of the eighteenth century, the civilian force acted mostly as a night-watch service, and military personnel remained responsible for defending the area.

In 1838, the Montreal Government Police Force was formed. It consisted of a police superintendent, two inspectors, and 122 officers. In 1843, the government gave up its supervising role, and the Montreal Police Force was created. As Montreal continued to grow, the force grew with it, adding more officers, police stations, and equipment. The twentieth century brought more changes and additions, including the first police car in 1913, the adoption of Canada's first drug squad in 1922, the swearing-in of female officers in 1947, and the 1972 creation of the Montreal Urban Community Police Department.

The civil police force turned into an official group of peace officers. The group disbanded in 1837.

Montreal's first female police officers joined in 1947.

Key Events

1840 Montreal receives its second city charter. The first Montreal police department is formed.

1844 Montreal becomes the capital of the United Province of Canada.

1849 Riots lead to the burning of the Parliament Building, ending Montreal's status as capital of the United Province of Canada.

Early Transportation

Montreal became a major port in the 1820s, when construction of the Lachine Canal was completed. This canal was built to bypass the wild Lachine rapids, which, for hundreds of years, had served as an obstacle to navigation on the St. Lawrence River. During the next twenty-five years, improvements were made to the canal, and Montreal became the principal seaport in the east. The Lachine Canal remained the city's primary shipping route until the St. Lawrence Seaway was opened in 1959.

A Separatist Movement

In the 1960s, a **resurgence** of French pride led to important achievements and reforms in French arts, industry, and politics. Labelled "The Quiet Revolution," this period stirred a powerful movement within the province. The number of **separatist** groups in Quebec increased, and Montreal became the site of several demonstrations. It also became the site of several terrorist attacks. Beginning in 1963, an **extremist** separatist group called the Front de Liberation de Quebec (FLQ) carried out a series of attacks against English businesses in Montreal. Then, in October of 1970, members of the FLQ kidnapped British diplomat James Cross and Quebec cabinet minister Pierre Laporte. In response to the kidnapping, the Federal Government sent the Canadian Armed Forces to Montreal. By the end of the October Crisis, Pierre Laporte had been found dead, and a number of the kidnappers had been apprehended. Since the crisis, separatism has remained a hotly debated and always-current issue in Quebec.

The St. Lawrence Seaway provides an avenue for international trade.

1867 Quebec, Ontario, New Brunswick, and Nova Scotia join together to form the country of Canada.

1881 The Canadian Pacific Railway establishes its headquarters in Montreal.

1920 The Royal Canadian Mounted Police establishes its headquarters in Montreal.

1967 Montreal hosts Expo 67.

Famous People

Pierre Trudeau 1919–2000

Pierre Trudeau was a respected lawyer, writer, professor, and politician. He was also one of Canada's best-known prime ministers. Born in Montreal, Pierre attended the Académie Querbes, and then went on to study at Jean-de-Brébeuf College. In the early 1940s, he earned a law degree from the University of Montreal and a Master's degree in political economy from Harvard. In 1965, Pierre joined the Liberal Party and was elected to Parliament. When Lester Pearson resigned as prime minister and leader of the Liberal party in 1968, Pierre decided to run for leadership of the party. He won, then immediately called a federal election. Pierre served as prime minister of Canada for sixteen years. In 1999, he was named the top Canadian newsmaker of the twentieth century.

Pierre Trudeau was instrumental in establishing Canada's multicultural policies.

Maurice Richard 1921–2000

Maurice "Rocket" Richard was one of Canada's most celebrated hockey players. Born in Montreal, Maurice began skating at the age of 4. In 1942, Maurice joined the Montreal Canadiens and played his first game in the National Hockey League. Maurice soon became the star of the team and one of the NHL's leading goal-scorers. He played with the Canadiens for a remarkable eighteen seasons, and his intensity and skill drew admiration from his fellow players and his many fans. Maurice was one of the most exciting hockey players of his generation. In the 1944-45 season, he became the first player in the NHL to score fifty goals in fifty games. In 1947, he won the prestigious Hart Trophy as the NHL's most valuable player.

Maurice Richard was inducted into the Hockey Hall of Fame in 1961.

Mordecai Richler 1931–2001

Mordecai Richler was one of Canada's most highly regarded writers. Born in Montreal, Mordecai took up residence in London, England, in 1954. In 1958, he published *The Apprenticeship of Duddy Kravitz*, a novel that has remained one of Canada's most celebrated literary works. Mordecai went on to write many more novels, including *Cocksure* (1968) and *Saint Urbain's Horseman* (1971), both of which won Governor General's Awards for literature. In 1972, he returned to Canada and from then on divided his time between England and Quebec. Among his many other popular novels are *Joshua Then and Now* (1980), *Solomon Gursky Was Here* (1989), and *Barney's Version* (1997), which won the prestigious Giller Prize.

Mordecai Richler was a Canadian literary legend.

Geneviève Bujold 1942–

Geneviève Bujold is a popular actor from Montreal. While enrolled in the Quebec Conservatory of Dramatic Art, Geneviève was offered a part in a professional production of a play entitled *The Barber of Seville*. Soon after, she was offered roles in many other productions. In 1969, Geneviève starred in *Anne of a Thousand Days*. Her performance in this film earned her a Golden Globe Award and an Academy Award nomination.

Geneviève Bujold has starred in films in Europe, Canada, and the United States.

Jeanne Mance 1606–1673

Jeanne Mance was among the group of French colonists that first came to settle at Ville Marie. Born in France, Jeanne lived with her father, Pierre Mance, until he died in 1640. After her father's death, Jeanne heard of plans to establish a colony on the island of Montreal. Jeanne decided that she would help to establish this colony. After a long journey, she and the rest of the group arrived at their destination on May 17, 1642. Upon her arrival, Jeanne founded a tiny hospital in her own home, where she attended to both European settlers and Native Peoples. In 1645, she founded Hôtel-Dieu, Montreal's very first official hospital.

Culture

The Arts

Montreal is known for its vibrant and diverse arts scene. The city is home to a wide variety of art galleries, theatre troupes, dance companies, musical groups, publishing houses, and film studios. It also has one of the oldest art museums in Canada—the Montreal Museum of Fine Arts. This museum houses a number of excellent collections that include prints, sculptures, and paintings by classical and present-day artists from Canada and around the world. Modern artwork by Canadian artists is also exhibited at the Museum of Contemporary Art. This museum is part of the Place des Arts complex, which has served as Montreal's main performing arts centre for more than thirty years.

Montreal has produced many celebrated performing artists. Among the countless musicians to come out of the city are jazz legends Oscar Peterson and Paul Bley, and singer/songwriter Leonard Cohen. Cohen, who has one of Canada's most recognizable voices, is also an admired poet and novelist. Other writers from Montreal include playwright Michel Tremblay, novelist Mavis Gallant, and poet Émile Nelligan. Cinema also thrives in the city. Many of the country's best-known film directors were born or have lived in Montreal.

In Old Montreal, artists gather to display and sell their creations.

FESTIVALS

Many of Montreal's most popular festivals and events are held during summer. The **International Fireworks Competition** takes place every June. This contest attracts competitors and spectators from around the world and features a number of breathtaking fireworks displays. The **International Jazz Festival** is also held in early summer. This ten-day festival is one of Montreal's most popular events. Many of North America's best jazz musicians perform at the festival, and dozens of free jazz concerts are staged throughout the city's downtown streets and plazas. In mid-July, Montreal hosts the **Just For Laughs Festival**. During this festival, hilarious comedy acts in English and French are performed at theatres around the

Celebrating the Holidays

Montrealers celebrate Saint-Jean–Baptiste Day with a series of concerts and parades.

Holidays in Montreal are celebrated with great energy. One of the liveliest celebrations in the city takes place on Saint-Jean–Baptiste Day. St. Jean Baptiste is the **patron** saint of French Canadians. Each year, on June 24, Montrealers of French descent honour their saint with a huge party that features bonfires, fireworks, dancing, music, and a parade. About one week later, more celebrating takes place—this time in honour of Canada's birthday. On July 1, Montreal holds a variety of Canada Day events, including a parade and musical performances.

In December, Montreal is lit up with numerous Christmas light displays. Festive activities, including Santa Claus parades and Nativity plays, take place throughout the city. At the Notre Dame Basilica, traditional Christmas carols are sung with the accompaniment of the Montreal Symphony Orchestra. Other choirs and carolers can be heard at many venues in the city. Once Christmas is over, Montrealers keep the festive spirit alive with Fête des Neiges. This event, which takes place during the first two weeks of February, celebrates the joys of winter. Families from all over the city gather at Notre-Dame Island to take part in activities such as tobogganing, snowshoeing, and ice skating. Ice-carving contests, bed races, and barrel jumping are also part of the fun.

city. Comedians from Quebec, the rest of Canada, and around the world travel to Montreal to take part in the event. At the end of summer, Montreal audiences can take in a wide variety of films during the **World Film Festival**. This festival brings several well-known film directors and movie stars to the city, and presents more than 400 films from 60 countries.

Fresh and Filling

People in Montreal like fresh food. The city is home to a range of shops and markets that sell fresh produce, meats, and dairy products from nearby farms. Atwater Market and Jean-Talon Market are among the city's most popular farmers' markets. Their indoor and outdoor stalls feature farm-fresh fruits and vegetables, as well as Quebec cheeses, game, maple syrup, and honey from local hives. Like most other Quebec towns and cities, Montreal offers its residents and visitors rich, hearty, French-Canadian cuisine. At the time of early French settlement in Quebec, meals consisted mostly of warm, filling foods that helped settlers get through cold, harsh winters. Ingredients included items that could be easily grown and harvested in the region, such as root vegetables, dried legumes, apples, maple syrup, and a variety of fish and game. Many of these ingredients are still used in today's French-Canadian cuisine. Among French Canada's many meal specialties are beans and pork baked in maple syrup, a meat pie called tourtière, and creton, a delicious spread made from spiced pork.

Fresh produce, meats, and dairy products have been available at Montreal's Atwater Market since 1933.

Montreal may be known for its rich, French cuisine, but an array of ethnic foods can also be found throughout the city. Montreal's Jewish community, for example, has introduced the city to smoked meat and bagels. There are also more than 4,000 restaurants in the city, many of which serve delicious ethnic meals, including Indian and Mediterranean dishes.

Poutine

- 1 package oven fries
- 2 packets gravy mix
- 1 L (4 cups) cheese curds
- 5 mL (1 tsp) salt
- 2 mL (1/2 tsp) pepper

Cook the fries according to the directions on the package. Prepare gravy, add salt and pepper, and set aside. Place fries in a large bowl, and cover with cheese curds. Pour gravy generously over fries and curds, allowing cheese to melt before eating.

Cultural Groups

Many of Montreal's French citizens are descended from the area's first settlers. Today, French culture thrives in the city. French-language theatres, newspapers, bookstores, and radio and television stations are found in abundance, and several organizations, museums, and festivals help to preserve and honour French traditions.

Many people of British ancestry live in Montreal as well. The city's first British settlers arrived in the eighteenth and nineteenth centuries. Today, about 10 percent of the people living in Montreal have British roots.

For the most part, Montreal's French and English inhabitants live in separate neighbourhoods. The city's main street, Saint Lawrence Boulevard, divides Montreal into west and east sections. Francophones live primarily on the east side of the street, while **Anglophones** live primarily on the west side.

Montreal is also home to several other cultural communities. Chinese people first came to the area in the late 1800s to work on the construction of the railway. Today, Montreal has a bustling Chinatown. More recent immigrants have come from other Asian countries, as well as the Caribbean Islands, South and Central America, and Africa. Montreal's Jewish population is also quite large, as are its Portuguese and Greek communities.

Many languages are spoken in Montreal's Chinatown, including French, English, Cantonese, Mandarin, and Vietnamese.

Language Tensions

For nearly 200 years, signs throughout Montreal were written in English, and most of the city's business was conducted in English as well. In the 1970s, the provincial government passed a series of language laws in an effort to preserve the French language. Among other things, these laws banned the use of English on public signage. Enforcement teams patrolled Montreal to ensure that no English was used on signs. Anglophones in the city saw this as a complete disregard for their rights. Since then, the signage law has been amended, but Montreal continues to struggle to find an acceptable balance between the use of its two main languages.

The Economy

A Centre of Industry

As one of Canada's largest cities, Montreal is an important centre for industry, commerce, and finance. Many of the country's largest and most powerful companies have their headquarters in Montreal. While the presence of several high-technology research firms has secured the city's position as a leader in technological development, Montreal companies also develop other products that contribute significantly to the city's income. Factories in metropolitan Montreal produce goods such as textiles and clothing, refined petroleum, processed foods and beverages, airplanes, rail cars, chemicals, tobacco products, electrical equipment, medicines, and metals.

Many of Montreal's goods are shipped to locations around the world via the city's port—one of Canada's busiest. Goods from other parts of the country, as well as other areas of the world, are also handled at the port, which offers the shortest route from central Canada to Europe and certain U.S. destinations. The city is also a centre for railway transportation. It still serves as the eastern headquarters for both the Canadian Pacific Railway and the Canadian National Railway. Several American railways service the city as well. Montreal's port and railway facilities have helped make the city a principal centre for national and international trade.

Items that come into Canada through Montreal's port include food products, iron ore, and petroleum.

The Service Sector

The majority of Montreal's workforce is employed in the service sector. The city's many service industries contribute the most to Montreal's annual income. People employed in the service sector help others. Service workers include doctors, caretakers, lawyers, teachers, and government employees. Those who work in one of the city's many financial institutions are also part of the service sector. Montreal is home to the head offices of some of Canada's largest banks, as well as many of its top insurance companies, brokerage houses, and investment firms.

More than 331,000 people are employed in Montreal's government and customer-service industries.

Another important facet of Montreal's service sector is tourism. Every year, millions of visitors from around the world travel to Montreal to take in its attractions and enjoy its cosmopolitan flare. The city has an extensive variety of hotels, restaurants, and shops to serve both visitors and residents. In fact, Montreal is famous for its abundance of restaurants and shopping areas, and for the high quality of the goods that these establishments offer. The city is known throughout the world as an important centre for both fashion and culture.

Every day, Montreal firefighters risk their lives to keep the city and its residents safe.

Métro trains in Montreal reach speeds of up to 72 km per hour.

Getting Around in Montreal

There are a number of ways to get around in Montreal. The city has an extensive road system that enables drivers to reach their destinations with ease. Montreal's major traffic artery is Saint Lawrence Boulevard. Known among locals as "The Main," this busy street crosses Montreal Island from north to south and carries a large portion of the city's traffic. Other busy streets in the city include Saint Denis and Saint Catherine streets, and René-Lévesque Boulevard.

More than 1.2 million people make use of Montreal's public transit system every day. Buses serve all parts of Montreal, and an efficient subway system, called Le Métro, consists of several lines that service various parts of the city. There are about sixty-five Métro stations in Montreal, and each is unique in its architectural design. The city also offers reliable commuter train service.

Years ago, Montreal's Métro system helped initiate what is now known as the Underground City. This "city" consists of a network of bustling underground passageways, linking many of Montreal's office buildings, railway and Métro stations, hotels, restaurants, and department stores. These extensive passageways run for about 29 km and serve more than 2,000 businesses. In the winter, Montrealers use these corridors, which are often lined with stores and eateries, to get from one point of the city to another without ever being exposed to the cold weather outside.

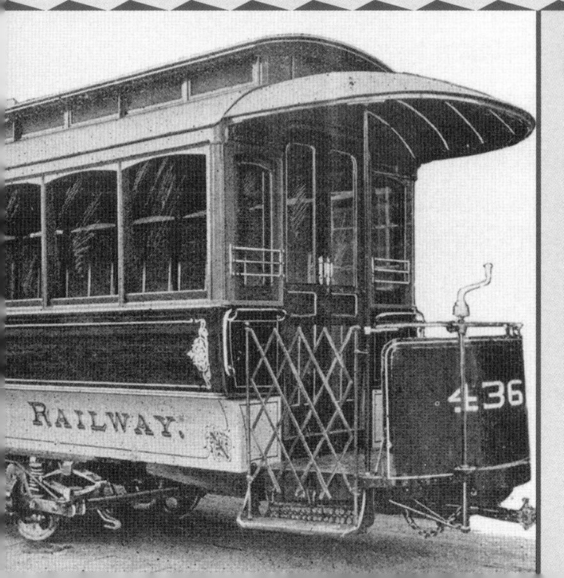

Horse-drawn Buses and Electric Streetcars

In 1861, the city created the Montreal City Passenger Railway Company. With about 12 km of railway track, 8 rail cars, and 14 horses, this company was the first in the city to offer public transportation services. Buses mounted on sleighs and pulled by horses replaced the company's rail cars in the winter. Montreal's first electric streetcar began operating in 1892. During the next 100 years, Montreal continued to add to and improve upon its public transportation system. Today, the Montreal Urban Community Transit Corporation oversees the maintenance and development of the city's first-rate Métro, bus, and train systems.

Learning and Research

Montreal is an important centre for education and research. The city has two public school systems to meet the needs of its residents. One system is for students who speak French, and the other is for students who speak English. In 1977, a law was passed to restrict access to English-language schools. Called the Charter of the French Language, or Bill 101, this law states that children of newly arrived immigrants to Montreal are required to enrol in French-language schools. The city also has a significant number of French and English private schools.

Montreal is home to four excellent universities.

Montreal is one of the country's leading centres for post-secondary education. The city is home to four excellent universities. McGill University and Concordia University provide mainly English-language instruction, while l'Université de Montréal and l'Université du Québec á Montréal provide instruction primarily in French. All four of Montreal's universities are internationally recognized for the high quality of their programs and for their groundbreaking research in a variety of fields. McGill University is one of the largest post-secondary institutions in Canada, and l'Université de Montréal is the largest French university outside of France.

More than 16,000 students study full-time at McGill University.

Sports and Recreation

Outdoor Fun

Montreal offers plenty of exciting opportunities for outdoor enthusiasts. The city has several municipal parks, where Montrealers and visitors can enjoy all kinds of activities. One of the largest and most frequented of these parks is Parc Mont-Royal, or Mount Royal Park. This beautiful expanse sits on top of the city's mountain and serves as a popular spot for hikers and cyclists, as well as birdwatchers and picnickers. Montreal also has an extensive network of trails for cyclists, joggers, walkers, and inline skaters. About 750 km of bicycle paths wind through the city and around Montreal Island. Trails along the Lachine Canal and Old Montreal are especially popular. The city also has many other outdoor facilities. Golfers in Montreal can choose from about 100 golf courses, and team-sports enthusiasts have access to 60 basketball courts, 474 soccer and football fields, and 975 baseball parks. For those who prefer water sports, Montreal has more than 600 sq km of waterways that can be used for activities such as swimming, sailing, or even white-water rafting.

Cycling is a fun way to enjoy the many sights of Montreal.

A terrace atop Mount Royal offers a spectacular view of Montreal.

Cheering on the Teams

Spectator sports are very popular in Montreal. The city is home to four professional sports teams, each of which receives a tremendous amount of support from their hometown fans. The Montreal Expos are one of two Canadian teams in the National Baseball League. Fans from around the province and across the country have cheered them on since they were founded in 1968. The Expos, who were named for the city's successful Expo 67, play their home games at the Olympic Stadium.

Montreal also boasts a professional football team. The Montreal Alouettes are part of the Canadian Football League. Whenever they play at home, thousands of fans come to cheer them on at Molson Stadium.

Montreal's most popular spectator sport is hockey. The Montreal Canadiens have been a part of the National Hockey League since 1909. This amazing team has won more championships than any other hockey team in North America and has produced some of the most popular players in the sport, including Maurice "Rocket" Richard, Jean Beliveau, and Guy Lafleur. The Canadiens play their home games at the newly constructed Molson Centre—the largest hockey arena in Canada.

The Montreal Canadiens won twenty-four Stanley Cup championships from 1916 to 1993.

Racing Action

Another popular spectator sport in Montreal is racing. The city is home to two first-rate racing facilities. The Hippodrome de Montreal, which is also known as the Blue Bonnets Racetrack, hosts a number of exciting horse-racing events every year, including the Breeder's Cup.

Racing of a different sort takes place on Notre-Dame Island. Every June, The Gilles-Villeneuve Circuit hosts the Formula One Grand Prix.

Tourism

Old Montreal

Old Montreal is a very popular tourist area. It is also the city's birthplace. In 1642, Paul de Chomedey, Sieur de Maisonneuve and his group of forty French colonists settled by the river in this area. The small community soon blossomed into a thriving city. Today, Old Montreal serves as a powerful reminder of the city's long and exciting history. It covers about 15 hectares and is framed by the Saint Lawrence River and McGill, Notre-Dame, and Berri streets. The area's narrow, cobblestone streets are lined with buildings that date back to the seventeenth, eighteenth, and nineteenth centuries. Many of these buildings are now occupied by shops, restaurants, and apartments, while others house fascinating museums that exhibit everything from antique dolls to artifacts relating to the city's history. Old Montreal is also home to a number of historic public squares.

One of the most visited areas of Old Montreal is the Old Port. This waterfront zone once accommodated the city's earliest commercial wharves. In the early 1990s, the Old Port was turned into a recreation area. Tourists and residents enjoy strolling down the 2.5 km waterfront walkway, which in summer is also crowded with cyclists, joggers, and inline skaters. Playgrounds and picnic areas are scattered throughout the Old Port, and a wide variety of outdoor entertainment is offered as well. Children's performers, buskers, an IMAX theatre, and a yacht harbour are all found in the Old Port. Visitors can also climb the 192 steps of the area's historic Clock Tower, which was constructed in 1922 and offers three observation decks, all of which supply great views of the city.

Old Montreal serves as a reminder of the city's long and exciting history.

The Old Port of Montreal underwent a restoration that was completed in 1992.

Olympic Park

Montreal's Olympic Park was built for the 1976 Summer Olympic Games. Located at the east end of the city, this massive sports complex provided Olympic athletes with excellent facilities, including a six-pool swimming complex and a velodrome for cycling. Today, Olympic Park is home to several other attractions that draw thousands of visitors every year. The Montreal Tower is part of the Olympic Stadium. It leans at a 45° angle and is the world's tallest inclined tower. Visitors can take a cable car to the top of the tower, where an observation deck provides 80-km views of Montreal and its surroundings.

The Olympic Stadium, in Montreal's Olympic Park, hosts concerts, exhibitions, and sporting events.

Montreal Botanical Gardens

The Montreal Botanical Garden is located just across the street from the Olympic Sports Complex. Built in 1931, this breathtaking garden has grown into one of the largest in the world. It contains more than ten greenhouses and thirty themed gardens. Among the most popular are the Chinese and Japanese gardens. The Chinese garden has plants and trees native to southern China, including a **pavilion** that features miniature trees. The Japanese Garden features ponds, streams, and bridges lined with Canadian plants arranged in traditional Japanese style. The Montreal Botanical Gardens has more than 25,000 types of plants.

The Insectarium is also located on the grounds of the garden. This museum houses insects from more than 100 countries. Its exhibits include mounted scarabs, maggots, locusts, beetles, and tarantulas. There are also live exhibits of butterflies, scorpions, tarantulas, cockroaches, and many other insects.

Island Fun

Montreal's Jean Drapeau Park is situated in the middle of the Saint Lawrence River. This exciting park is made up of Sainte Hélène and Notre-Dame islands, which together served as the site of Expo 67, an enormous international fair held in Montreal in 1967. At this fair, more than sixty nations exhibited their cultures in pavilions located on the two islands. Although most of the pavilions are no longer there, the islands have several other attractions that continue to draw visitors. Notre-Dame Island boasts floral gardens, a sandy beach, a casino, the Olympic Basin, and the Gilles-Villeneuve Circuit.

Costumed soldiers re-enact historical events at the Sainte Hélène Fort.

On Sainte Hélène Island, tourists can visit the Sainte Hélène Fort, which was built in the nineteenth century to protect Montreal against possible aggression from the United States. The fort houses the David M. Stewart Museum, which displays military artifacts, maps, and models relating to the history of Montreal.

Perhaps the most popular summer attraction on Sainte Hélène Island is La Ronde Amusement Park. This park was built for Expo 67 but has changed considerably since then due to the addition of state-of-the-art rides. La Ronde has more than thirty-five rides, including Le Monstre, which is the world's tallest wooden roller coaster, and Le Cobra, which tackles a 360° loop while its riders are standing up!

Each year, Sainte Hélène Island attracts thousands of visitors from around the world.

Just For Laughs

Montreal is home to the world's very first museum devoted to comedy and laughter. Established in 1993, the Just for Laughs Museum explores the many different aspects and types of humour. One of the most popular exhibits at the museum is called "The Entertainers." This interactive exhibit is especially for children and features plays about clowns, puppets, and street performers who have entertained audiences since the sixteenth century. Once visitors have completed their historical journey, they are guided to a real stage, where they can learn all about the world of theatre. Children are invited to play with theatrical props and discover the joys of performing.

Montreal offers many attractions for those interested in outer space.

The Space Centre

Tourists interested in the science of the stars will find plenty to do in Montreal. Located in the heart of the city's downtown, the Montreal Planetarium lets visitors explore the wonders of outer space through fascinating interactive exhibits. The planetarium's main attraction is the Theatre of the Stars. This enormous theatre, with its 20 m high dome, presents a variety of shows throughout the year. These informative and exciting presentations cover a range of topics, from space travel to time travel, as well as the exploration of stars and planets.

The Cosmodome is another excellent place for visitors to learn more about the mysteries of the universe. Located in the northern Montreal suburb of Laval, the Cosmodome has captivating exhibits and interactive displays devoted to topics such as the moon, the solar system, and the forces that shaped Earth's evolution. A multimedia presentation called "Reach for the Stars" describes humankind's historic achievements in the discovery of the cosmos, astronomy, and space exploration. The Cosmodome also has a popular space camp for children.

Architecture

Historic Cathedrals

As one of Canada's oldest and largest cities, Montreal has some of the most stunning architecture in the country. Countless examples of modern architecture can be seen in the city's impressive skyscrapers, hotels, shops, and public squares. While many of Montreal's modern structures have received praise for their impressive designs, the city's older structures tend to draw the most attention and appreciation. Montreal has maintained many of its historic buildings from the seventeenth century onwards. Among the city's most remarkable buildings are its many churches and cathedrals. Notre-Dame Basilica, in Old Montreal, is one of the largest churches in Canada. Built between 1824 and 1829, it is considered a masterpiece of **Gothic Revival** architecture. The interior of Notre-Dame Basilica, which seats up to 4,000 people, is beautifully decorated. Its furnishings are carved mostly from wood that is delicately **gilded** and painted. Notre-Dame also houses a symphonic organ with 5,772 pipes, one of the world's largest bells, and 11 stained-glass windows that depict scenes from the Bible. Saint Joseph's Oratory is another impressive basilica in Montreal. Built in 1904, it sits on top of Mount Royal and has a 97 m copper dome, the world's second tallest, after Saint Peter's Basilica in Rome, Italy.

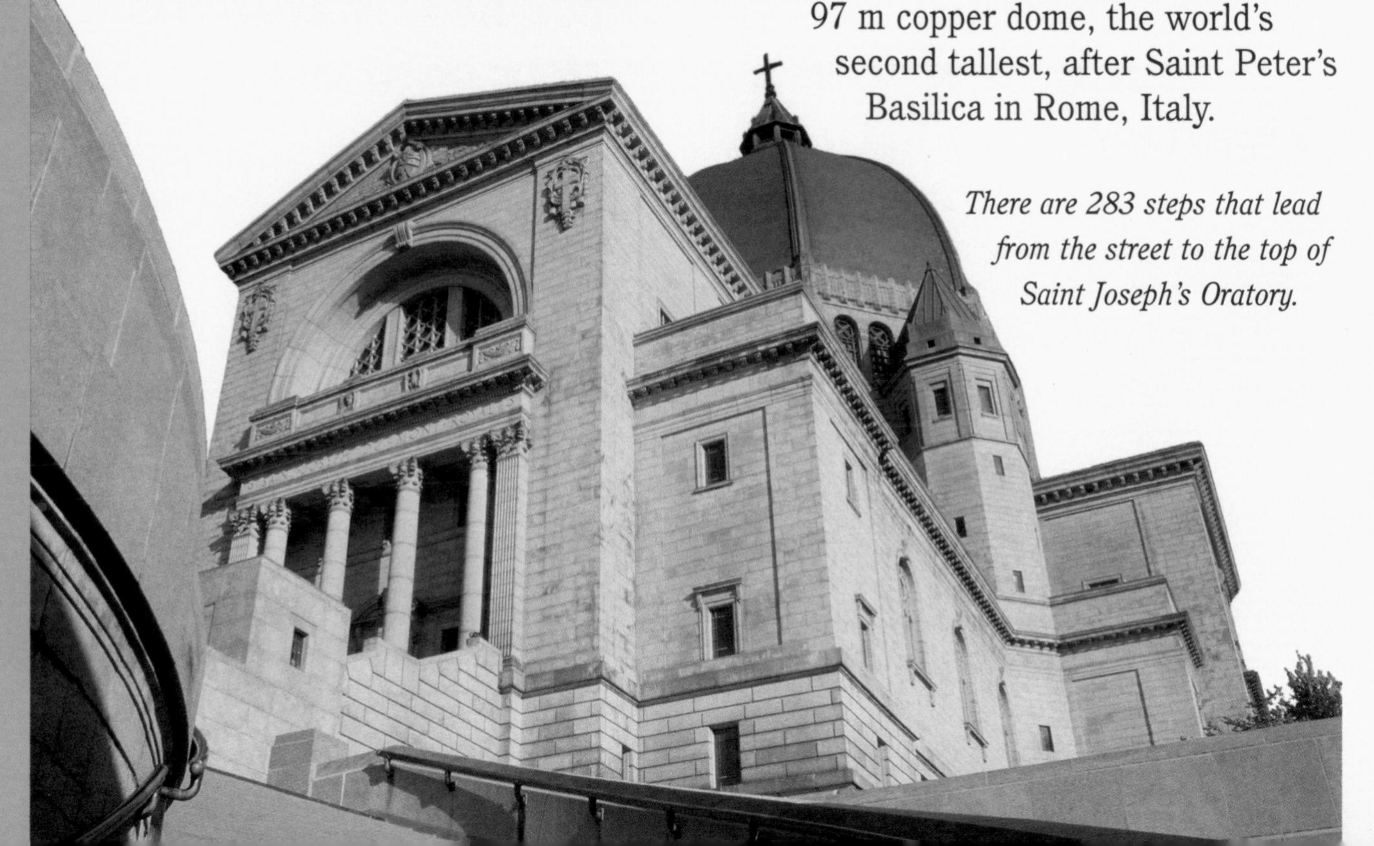

There are 283 steps that lead from the street to the top of Saint Joseph's Oratory.

Buildings for the Government

Many of Montreal's historic buildings were constructed to house various branches of the city's government. One of the oldest structures in the city is the Château Ramezay. Completed in 1705, the château was constructed for Claude de Ramezay who was, at that time, the governor of Montreal. The château served as a home for the governor and his family, and then later as a home for various other French colonial administrators. After the British gained control of Montreal, the château served as the British Government House until the mid-nineteenth century. In the 1890s, it was made into a museum, and today it houses a rich collection of furniture, clothing, and other artifacts from the eighteenth and nineteenth centuries.

In 1929, Château Ramezay became the first building to be classified a historical monument by the Quebec government.

Canadian Centre for Architecture

The Canadian Centre for Architecture is both a museum and a centre for the study of architecture. This centre is devoted to presenting and interpreting the art of architecture through historic and modern collections of architectural plans, drawings, models, books, and photographs. The main building of the Canadian Centre for Architecture houses exhibition rooms, a lecture theatre, a library, restoration and preservation galleries, and a bookstore. Designed and constructed in the late 1980s, the building itself has won many architectural awards in the United States and in Europe. Montreal's historic Shaughnessy House is also part of the Canadian Centre for Architecture. Classified as a historic monument by the provincial and federal governments, this enormous nineteenth-century home features a conservatory as well as grand reception rooms that are open to the public.

Fascinating Facts

1

Before 1966, Notre-Dame Island did not exist. It was created from the millions of tonnes of rock and dirt that were dug out from underneath Montreal's downtown streets during the construction of the Métro. The dirt and rock were dumped into the St. Lawrence River, next to Sainte Hélène Island, and soon the city had a new island on which it could build pavilions and other attractions for Expo 67.

2

In the early days of French settlement in Montreal, there were more male settlers than there were female settlers. By 1655, more than 700 single men lived in the colony, while only 65 single women called the area home. In order to solve the problem, King Louis XIV of France granted **dowries** to French orphan girls who then travelled to the colony to marry. Soon, more than 700 "Daughters of the King" were living in Montreal.

3

Montreal's Saint Suplice Seminary was built in 1684, making it the oldest surviving building in the city. The clock on the building's tower, which is made almost entirely of wood, dates from 1701. It is believed to be one of the oldest public clocks in North America.

4

In 1893, the Montreal AAA became the very first hockey team to win the prestigious Stanley Cup.

5

The illuminated cross that sits on the summit of Mount Royal serves as an important marker for Montreal builders. A city bylaw forbids downtown developers to build skyscrapers that rise higher than the cross.

6

In 1956, Montrealer Lucille Wheeler became the first Canadian to win an Olympic medal in skiing—a bronze in downhill. Two years later, she became the first North American to win a world championship in both downhill and giant slalom.

7

In 1904, a religious man by the name of Brother André built a small chapel near the future site of the Saint Joseph Oratory. This chapel was meant to honour Saint Joseph, Canada's patron saint. It became known that Brother André had healing powers, and soon people were travelling from around the world to be healed by "The Miracle Man of Montreal." Donations from healed patients helped fund the construction of the Saint Joseph Oratory, which was built about thirty years after Brother André's death. Today, his heart is on display in a glass case at the basilica's museum.

8

Many of the buildings in Montreal's residential neighbourhoods have winding, outdoor staircases. Some of these staircases were built in order to save space inside crowded homes.

9

Montreal is home to one of the largest and most successful circuses in the world. Since 1984, the Cirque du Soleil has wowed audiences with its amazing performances. The Cirque presents a variety of talented acrobats, dancers, clowns, trapeze artists, tightrope walkers, and **contortionists**. It has performed for more than 30 million people worldwide, and now employs about 2,100 people.

10

During the 1980s, archaeological digs in Old Montreal unearthed many historic treasures left behind by the city's earliest settlers. Original street pavements and foundations, brick sewer pipes, and even a cemetery were buried beneath the city, where they remained undiscovered for hundreds of years. Today, the Montreal Museum of Archaeology and History sits on the site. Visitors to the museum can go underground and explore the many items that were unearthed during the digs.

Activities

Based on what you have read, try to answer the following questions.

Multiple Choice

1 What was the name of the very first European settlement in Montreal?

a. Hochelaga
b. Ville Marie
c. Place Royale
d. Pointe-à-Callière

2 Which of the following is the oldest surviving building in Montreal?

a. Château Ramezay
b. Notre-Dame Basilica
c. Bonsecours Market
d. Saint Suplice Seminary

3 Which Montreal sports team plays its home games at the Olympic Stadium?

a. The Canadiens
b. The Alouettes
c. The Expos
d. all of the above

4 Who founded the very first hospital in Montreal?

a. Paul de Chomedey, Sieur de Maisonneuve
b. Jeanne Mance
c. Jacques Cartier
d. King Louis XIV of France

5 Who wrote *Solomon Gursky Was Here*?

a. Pierre Trudeau
b. Mordecai Richler
c. Geneviève Bujold
d. Jacques Viger

True or False

6 The Lachine Canal has served as Montreal's primary shipping route since the early 1800s.

7 In 1945, Maurice Richard became the first player in the NHL to score forty points in forty games.

8 Montreal has a thriving mini-city beneath its surface.

9 The Montreal Tower is the world's tallest tower.

10 Montreal is home to the world's tallest wooden roller coaster.

Answers:
1. b.
2. d.
3. c.
4. b.
5. b.
6. False. It was closed after the Saint Lawrence Seaway was opened in 1959. The Seaway has served as the primary shipping route since then.
7. False. He became the first player to score fifty goals in fifty games.
8. True. It is known as the Underground City.
9. False. It is considered the world's tallest inclined tower.
10. True. Called Le Monstre, it is found in La Ronde Amusement Park.

More Information

Books

Craats, Rennay. **Eye on Canada: Quebec.** Calgary: Weigl Educational Publishers, 2001.

Symon, John. **The Lobster Kids' Guide to Exploring Montreal.** Montreal: Lobster Press, 2000.

Rogers, Stillman D. **Montreal**. New York: Children's Press, 2000.

Web sites

Montreal Tourism
http://www.tourism-montreal.org

Guide to Montreal
http://www.pagemontreal.qc.ca

Cirque du Soleil
http://www.cirquedusoleil.com

Just for Laughs Museum
http://www.hahaha.com

Montreal Planetarium
http://www.planetarium.montreal.qc.ca

La Ronde Amusement Park
http://www.laronde.com

Olympic Park
http://www.rio.gouv.qc.ca

Some Web sites stay current longer than others. To find information on Montreal, use your Internet search engine to look up topics such as "Bonsecours Market," "Expo 67," "Maurice Richard," or any other topic you want to research.

Glossary

Anglophones: people who speak English

charter: a written contract or constitution

confluence: a place where two or more rivers meet

contortionists: people who can bend and twist their bodies in unusual ways

diversity: cultural variety

dowries: the money and goods brought by wives to their husbands

extremist: a person who goes beyond accepted limits

Francophones: people who speak French

gilded: covered with gold

Gothic Revival: a style of architecture that makes use of pointed arches and vaults

palisaded: fenced

patron: one who protects or supports

pavilion: a tent or building that houses exhibits

resurgence: a revival or return to activity

separatist: a person who wishes to be independent of a place or association

Index